LEARNING
TO STUDY THE
BIBLE

L. J. Zimmerman

Leader Guide

Abingdon Press
Nashville

LEARNING TO STUDY THE BIBLE

EDITORIAL / DESIGN TEAM

Erin R. Floyd . . . . Editor
Madeline Walls . . . . Production Editor
Kent Sneed . . . . Designer

ADMINISTRATIVE TEAM

Rev. Brian K. Milford . . . . . . .President and Publisher
Marjorie M. Pon. . . Associate Publisher and Editor of Church School Publications (CSP)
Mary M. Mitchell . . . . .Design Manager
Brittany Sky . . . . Senior Editor, Children's Resources

Written by: L. J. Zimmerman

Cover Design: Kellie Green; **Art:** Shutterstock®

LEARNING TO STUDY THE BIBLE: LEADER GUIDE. An official resource for The United Methodist Church approved by Discipleship Ministries and published by Abingdon Press, a division of The United Methodist Publishing House, 2222 Rosa L. Parks Blvd., Nashville, TN 37228-1306. Price: $14.99. Copyright © 2018 Abingdon Press. All rights reserved. Printed in the United States of America.

For information concerning permission to reproduce any material in this publication, write to Rights and Permissions, The United Methodist Publishing House, 2222 Rosa L. Parks Blvd., Nashville, TN 37228-1306. You may fax your request to 615-749-6128. Or email permissions@umpublishing.org.

If you have questions or comments, call toll free: 800-672-1789. Or email customerhelp@cokesbury.com.

To order copies of this publication, call toll free: **800-672-1789.** You may fax your order to 800-445-8189. Telecommunication Device for the Deaf/Telex Telephone: 800-227-4091. Or order online at **cokesbury.com.** Use your Cokesbury account, American Express, Visa, Discover, or MasterCard.

Scripture quotations are taken from the Common English Bible. Copyright © 2011 by the Common English Bible. All rights reserved. Used by permission.

18 19 20 21 22 23 24 25 26 27—10 9 8 7 6 5 4 3 2 1

ISBN: 9781501871078
PACP10541720-01

How to Use Learning to Study the Bible

LEARNING TO STUDY THE BIBLE explores biblical history and methods of interpretation. It gives participants the tools they need to explore the Bible using the classic questions: Who? What? When? Where? Why? and How?

The primary component of LEARNING TO STUDY THE BIBLE is the Participant Book. Leaders guide participants in conducting their own Bible studies using their Participant Books. The leader's role is to introduce ideas, ask questions, and keep the group on track.

You will lead a group through the Participant Book over the course of eight sessions. Each session has three parts: Explore, Study, and Reflect.

1. **Explore:** Participants engage in an opening activity to begin conversation about the topic. They then move to foundational information and inquiry as they gain new insights.

2. **Study:** Participants take the concept they've explored and apply it to the Bible. They study a Bible story or passage together, and use the appropriate Bible study resources and tools (see pages 5–6) to deepen their understandings.

3. **Reflect:** After studying the text, the participants engage in individual reflection and then reflect as a group.

Studying the Bible is an exciting process. Remember, the journey of Bible study is lifelong. You don't need to have all the answers! You just need to be open to investigating this sacred text with your group. Use Prepare (p. 7) and the introduction of the Participant Book to reflect and to ready your group for this holy work. Also, *before the first session it is suggested to give group members their Participant Books. Before each session, participants and you, are encouraged to read, "Why does this matter?" in their books.*

Bible Study Resources

As you embark on this Bible study journey, you'll discover that there are many Bible study tools to choose from. Navigating the multitude of commentaries, dictionaries, concordances, and other tools can be confusing.

Each lesson in this study uses certain types of Bible study tools to investigate a text. It can be tempting to search online for free versions of these resources. Yet, the resources that are available online are not always compatible with the assumptions of this study (see page 7). Not every free commentary, for example, uses historical criticism to study the Bible. Not every Bible handbook encourages readers to look at the text from several angles.

Because we know it is difficult to find and access helpful Bible study tools, we have created a website where you can access the relevant pages of our CEB Bible study resources for most lessons.

Simply visit *deepbluekids.com/learningtostudy* and download the file corresponding to the session number. Each file contains content relevant to that session from the *CEB Study Bible, CEB Student Bible, CEB Bible Dictionary, CEB Concise Concordance,* and the *Abingdon New Interpreter's Bible Commentary.* This download is FREE.

Another useful, free resource is your local public library. Many libraries carry Bible study resources, including commentaries, handbooks, dictionaries, and so forth. Following is a list of recommended resources to use in conjunction with this study.

Common English Bible Resources

We believe that the Common English Bible (CEB) is the most responsibly translated, easy-to-read English version of the Bible. We recommend using the CEB translation whenever reading the Bible with your participants, as well as the additional CEB resources that can be accessed on our website. The CEB Bible study resources are listed below.

- ○ *The CEB Study Bible.* Edited by Joel B. Green. Nashville: Common English Bible, 2011.
- ○ *The CEB Student Bible.* Edited by Elizabeth Corrie. Nashville: Common English Bible, 2015.
- ○ *The CEB Navigation Bible.* Nashville: Common English Bible, 2018.
- ○ *The CEB Women's Bible.* Edited by Jaime Clark-Soles. Nashville: Common English Bible, 2016.
- ○ *The Common English Bible: Bible Dictionary.* Nashville: Common English Bible, 2011.
- ○ *The Common English Bible: Concise Concordance.* Nashville: Common English Bible, 2011.

Free Bible Study Resources

Scan this code to download FREE sample pages from the *CEB Study Bible, CEB Student Bible, CEB Bible Dictionary, CEB Concise Concordance,* and the *Abingdon New Interpreter's Bible Commentary.* You'll find all the relevant pages for each session, so your group can study the Bible with the help of trustworthy scholarship, for free! (If you don't have a QR code reader, type *deepbluekids.com/learningtostudy* into your browser.)

Recommended Commentaries

○ *The New Interpreter's Bible One-Volume Commentary*. Edited by Beverly Roberts Gaventa and David Petersen. Nashville: Abingdon Press, 2010.

○ *The Women's Bible Commentary*. Edited by Carol A. Newsom, Sharon H. Ringe, and Jacqueline E. Lapsley. 3rd ed. Louisville: Westminster John Knox Press, 2012.

○ *HarperCollins Bible Commentary*. By the Society of Biblical Literature, edited by James L Mays. Rev. ed. San Francisco: HarperOne, 2000.

○ *The Oxford Bible Commentary*. Edited by John Barton and John Muddiman. Oxford: Oxford University Press, 2001.

○ *The IVP Bible Background Commentary: Old Testament*. Edited by John H. Walton, Victor H. Matthews, and Mark W. Chavalas. Downers Grove, IL: InterVarsity Press, 2000.

○ *The IVP Bible Background Commentary: New Testament*. Edited by Craig S. Keener. Downers Grove, IL: InterVarsity Press, 2014.

Recommended Bible Handbooks

○ *The Essential Bible Handbook*. Nashville: Abingdon Press, 2009.

○ *The Complete Bible Handbook: An Illustrated Companion,* by John Bowker. New York: DK Publishing, 2001.

○ *The Eerdmans Companion to the Bible*. Edited by Gordon D. Fee and Robert L. Hubbard, Jr., Grand Rapids: Wm. B. Eerdmans Publishing Co., 2011.

○ *The Oxford Companion to the Bible*. Edited by Bruce M. Metzger and Michael D. Coogan. Oxford: Oxford University Press, 2004.

Recommended Bible Dictionaries (Non-CEB)

○ *HarperCollins Bible Dictionary*. By the Society of Biblical Literature, edited by Mark Allan Powell. Revised and updated. 3rd ed. San Francisco: HarperOne, 2011.

○ *Eerdmans Dictionary of the Bible*. Edited by David Noel Freedman. Grand Rapids: Wm. B. Eerdmans Publishing Co., 2000.

Prepare

The goal of **LEARNING TO STUDY THE BIBLE** is to equip participants to read and study the Bible for themselves. It seeks to deepen one's understandings of the biblical stories and to help participants grow in their biblical faith. **LEARNING TO STUDY THE BIBLE** explores the basic questions of interpretation: what is the Bible, and what does it mean to me?

This curriculum is written with several assumptions about the Bible:

○ The Bible is a living text. While it was written hundreds or thousands of years ago, it continues to speak to people of faith today, and is interpreted in a variety of contexts and cultures.

○ The Bible was created in a historical context very different from our own. Learning about the historical context of the Bible and its authors enriches our understanding of the text.

○ Biblical interpretation is an act of faith, guided by the Holy Spirit.

○ Every reader has interpretive lenses, ways of seeing the world that affect his or her interpretation of the text.

○ There are many interpretive layers between ourselves and the biblical text, in the form of translators, scribes, copyists, editors, authors, and oral storytellers.

Take a moment to consider what you think about these assumptions. Which of them strike you? What assumptions about the Bible do you bring to this study?

The Bible is an important book in Western culture. References to the Bible abound in books, movies, and popular culture. There are many different teachings, both explicit and implicit, about what the Bible is and why it matters to our lives. Some of those teachings have been damaging to people of faith. What were you taught about the Bible growing up? Did you find your education about the Bible helpful? Why or why not?

Differing interpretations of the Bible have fueled many bitter fights among Christians over the centuries. Even the formation of the biblical canon (the list of books accepted as Holy Scripture) caused a stir! What are some controversial topics that come up for you when you think about studying the Bible? How can you respond in a loving, encouraging way?

Take some time to pray for the group members in your Bible study. If you know who will be participating, list their names here. Remember that God is big enough to handle all our questions, all our doubts, and all our wrestling with the Bible.

Who? Author and Audience

Why does this matter?

For some Bibles sold online, the author is listed as God. This reference to the divine inspiration of the sacred Scriptures is amusing, but it clouds an important reality. God's word comes to us through real people. The people who created the Scriptures as we know them were humans like us: people who told the stories of their faith, wrote them down, edited them, compiled them, and painstakingly copied them over the centuries. The people who created the Bible were deeply invested in their own faith, and in passing on their traditions to others.

What we find in the Bible is the embodied Word of God—embodied by those who originally spoke and wrote the words. God's truth comes to us in human-shaped containers. The humans bearing God's word spoke certain languages, had particular beliefs about the world, and had relationships with their original audiences. Much of that information is lost to us. But what we can discover about the authors of the Scriptures enriches our understanding of the words.

Sometimes the Bible itself tells us about its authors. Psalm 51 is attributed to King David, for example. This psalm of contrition is much more meaningful because we can read up on the back-story (2 Samuel 11–12). Paul's letter to the Philippians is made richer by knowing the story of Paul founding the Philippian church with Lydia (Acts 16:11-40).

In other instances, our ability to get to know the author is guesswork, based on the text itself. The Book of Isaiah, for example, is suspected to be composed by three different individuals, then compiled into one prophetic book. Biblical scholars identify these three "Isaiahs" by their writing style, the historical references they include, and the themes they take up. Knowing that the original Isaiah wrote from a crumbling Israelite kingdom, while a later "ghostwriter" wrote from the Babylonian exile, gives the text new shades of meaning.

Knowledge of the people who wrote and received the Bible is one part of interpretation. However, God's word continues to speak in new contexts today. By connecting, even in a small way, with the humans on the other side of the stories, Scripture comes to life in a new way.

Supplies

- Bibles (CEB)
- Bible dictionary (CEB)
- Participant Book
- sticky notes
- pens, pencils, colored pencils, markers
- dry-erase board and marker set or a large piece of paper

Learning Goals

- Learn about the authors and original audiences of the Bible
- Use a Bible dictionary
- Sharpen deductive reasoning skills in biblical interpretation

Helping Participants

You may think you need to have all the answers in order to do an in-depth Bible study. I've got good news for you: you don't! In fact, it is likely people prefer it if you avoid giving the answers. Instead, let participants explore and come to their own understandings. Your job is to ask good questions, facilitate conversation, and to help keep the group on track.

Participants may feel hesitant on opening up their curiosity and questions about the Bible. Often, adults need encouragement training their curiosity on the Bible. If they've been discouraged from questioning in the past, or taught that there is only one correct interpretation of a given Bible story, they may feel afraid to explore and ask questions. However, you are a guide for the journey, and remind them that you have questions as well and want to learn more. Bring your own questions about the Bible and faith and learn to explore these topics together.

Explore

OPEN IT UP

○ Before class, make sticky notes with the name of a famous person for each participant. Suggested names include: George Washington, Elvis Presley, Albert Einstein, Queen Elizabeth, Walt Disney, J. K. Rowling, Martin Luther King Jr., and so forth.

○ As people arrive, place a sticky note on their backs. Make sure the participant does not see the name written on the sticky note.

○ Begin class by inviting everyone to mingle with one another, asking yes-or-no questions to find out their identities.

○ Once a person has discovered their identity, invite them to sit down.

○ **ASK:** What information helped you discover which famous person you were? How might we apply these techniques to exploring the authors of the Bible?

---

lost to us. But what we can discover about the authors of the Scriptures enriches our understanding of the words.

Sometimes the Bible itself tells us about its authors. Psalm 51 is attributed to King David, for example. This psalm of contrition is much more meaningful because we can read up on the backstory (2 Samuel 11–12). Paul's letter to the Philippians is made richer by knowing the story of Paul founding the Philippian church with Lydia (Acts 16:11-40).

In other instances, our ability to get to know the author is guesswork based on the text itself. The Book of Isaiah, for example, is suspected to be composed by three different individuals, then compiled into one prophetic book. Biblical scholars identify these three "Isaiahs" by their writing style, the historical references they include, and the themes they take up. Knowing that the original Isaiah wrote from a crumbling Israelite kingdom, while a later "ghostwriter" wrote from the Babylonian exile, gives the text new shades of meaning.

Knowledge of the people who wrote and received the Bible is one part of interpretation. However, God's word continues to speak in new contexts today. By connecting, even in a small way, with the humans on the other side of the stories, Scripture comes to life in a new way.

Who Wrote the Bible

Let's start with the basics. The Bible isn't just one book. It's actually a collection of books—like a library. The Bible includes sixty-six books. Does that mean there were sixty-six authors of the Bible? Not exactly.

8

EXPLORE

○ Open It Up
○ Foundations

STUDY

○ Read a Text
○ Biblical Tools

Who? Author and Audience

Some books are collections of stories that used to be passed down orally. Before they were written down, people told the stories around fires, at meals, and before bed. The stories were well-known, and everyone told them in a slightly different way. It would be nearly impossible to identify the true author of these stories. Instead, we call the person who wrote all the stories down the editor.

Another thing that makes it hard to tell exactly how many people wrote the Bible is the use of pseudonyms. Pseudonyms are false names. People might use the name of a more famous person to give their writing more credibility. One example is in the Book of Ecclesiastes. The author claims to be a king of Israel, implying King Solomon, who was known for his wisdom. But evidence suggests that the book was probably written hundreds of years after King Solomon lived.

Pseudonyms weren't always meant to deceive people. Sometimes a prophet gathered followers who learned from the prophet and began to think and speak like the prophet. After the prophet's death, his followers might continue writing under his name. This wasn't considered lying or false. They were simply carrying on the prophet's train of thought. Parts of the Book of Isaiah are thought to be written by one of Isaiah's followers, years after Isaiah first preached.

There is sometimes little we can know about the people who wrote the Bible, but some things we can say with certainty. The people who wrote the Bible had powerful encounters with God. Their lives were changed by their faith, and they wanted to pass their faith on to future generations.

9

FOUNDATIONS

○ If they haven't already done so, allow time for participants to read "Why Does This Matter?" in the Participant Book. (It is encouraged for participants to read this section before the group meets).

○ Invite participants to read "Who Wrote the Bible" in their Participant Book.

○ Invite group members to share their initial responses or questions.

○ Write responses on the white board or a large piece of paper. Revisit these thoughts as you further explore the topic.

○ **ASK:** What questions do you have about the people who created and wrote the Bible?

REFLECT

○ Respond

○ Discuss

Study

READ A TEXT

○ Have group members find Acts 7:54–8:3, Acts 9:1-20, and 2 Corinthians 11:22-27 in their Bibles. Read the Scripture together.

○ **ASK:** How does the information you learned about Paul affect how you read these passages? Who is Paul writing to? What can you tell about Timothy from these passages?

BIBLICAL TOOLS

○ Look Up Timothy 1:3-14 in the Bible. Read the passage together.

○ Invite the participants to look up Paul/Saul and Timothy in a Bible dictionary.

○ **ASK:** What did you learn about Paul? about Timothy?

○ **SAY:** Bible dictionaries compile important information about Bible people, so you don't have to read every verse about them to make a profile.

BIBLICAL TOOLS
- Read: Acts 7:54–8:3, Acts 9:1-20, and 2 Corinthians 11:22-27.
- Look up Paul/Saul and Timothy in a Bible dictionary.
- Make notes about what you learned about Paul and Timothy.

How does the information you learned about Paul affect how you read these passages?

What difference does it make if you know about the people who wrote the Bible?

10

CLOSING PRAYER

Loving God, be our guide. With each question we ask and with every Scripture we read, may we rely on your Spirit as we more deeply explore your Holy Bible. Amen.

NOTES

11

Reflect

RESPOND

○ Invite participants to spend some time in individual reflection, responding to questions in the Participant Book.

DISCUSS

○ Invite participants to share their responses as they feel comfortable.

○ Return to the initial questions and responses written on the white board or large piece of paper. Consider new insights or perspectives. Discuss any remaining questions.

○ **ASK:** Do you think Paul realized that his letters would become sacred Scripture? Do you think he would have written any differently if he had?

○ Invite participants to take home their Participant Books and to read "Why Does This Matter?" for session 2 during the week.

Closing Prayer

Loving God, be our guide. With each question we ask and with every Scripture we read, may we rely on your Spirit as we more deeply explore your Holy Word. Amen.

Notes

What? Genre

Why does this matter?

In the 1999 movie *Galaxy Quest,* the washed-up stars of a popular 1970s science fiction show are visited by aliens. The aliens beam the actors into their spaceship and explain that they've discovered their "historical documents" and have proudly modeled their society after them. What they've really discovered are reruns of the science fiction show. They've made a mistake in genre.

It's an easy mistake to make. The television show is a broadcast from another society, in another time and place. But as this lighthearted comedy illustrates, making a mistake in genre can skew one's entire interpretation. Modern readers of the Bible face a similar challenge. We have stories and writings that have come to us from another society, in another time and place. One of the first major questions we face when trying to interpret these texts is that of genre.

Some examples of biblical genres include: poetry, worship songs, historical records, parables, narratives, satire, letters, and apocalyptic literature. Each genre has its own forms and style by which it is identified. Biblical poetry often uses parallelism, hyperbole, and metaphors. Letters often identify the author and audience in the first lines. Historical records list kings and events.

Some genres are easier to identify than others. Satire, for example, is often tricky. Think of how many people post articles on social media from satirical news websites without realizing they aren't true—and those are articles from our own time and place! Bible readers have even more difficulty identifying certain genres because of our lack of familiarity with the social and literary conventions of biblical societies.

Because of those barriers, we often must rely on biblical scholars who have researched other ancient writings to help us identify genre. However, you don't have to become experts in the forms of biblical case law to understand the Ten Commandments. The important thing is to simply recognize that genre matters and know how to investigate biblical genres.

Supplies

- Study Bibles (CEB, KJV)
- Bible dictionary (CEB)
- Bible commentary
- Participant Book
- pens, pencils, colored pencils, markers, paper
- basket
- dry-erase board and marker set or large piece of paper

Learning Goals

- Introduce and explore biblical genres
- Learn to use Bible commentaries and study Bibles to identify possible genres of texts
- Explore the significance of genre for biblical interpretation

Helping Participants

You may think you need to have all the answers in order to do an in-depth Bible study. I've got good news for you: you don't! In fact, it is likely people prefer it if you avoid giving the answers. Instead, let participants explore and come to their own understandings. Your job is to ask good questions, facilitate conversation, and to help keep the group on track

You and others are likely only to hear the word *genre* when thinking about English class. It's possible that you may not have made the connection between interpreting classic novels and interpreting other texts—from the Bible to the ads that pop up as you browse the web. Everything has a genre. Some of us have been taught that the Bible is one book with only one genre. Remind participants that the Bible is full of many different kinds of writings, and God speaks to us in many ways. Remind the group that it's amazing to have these ancient writings passed down to us, and it's our job to read them carefully and to try to interpret them as best we can.

Explore

OPEN IT UP

○ As people arrive, have each person write down his or her favorite book title, movie title, book quote, or movie quote, and place it in the basket.

○ Once everyone has arrived, invite each person to draw a piece of paper from the basket.

○ Take turns reading the answers and guessing the genre of the book or movie, based on what is written down.

○ **ASK:** How did you identify the genre?

Some examples of biblical genres include: poetry, worship songs, historical records, parables, narratives, satire, letters, and apocalyptic literature. Each genre has its own forms and style by which it is identified. Biblical poetry often uses parallelism, hyperbole, and metaphors. Letters often identify the author and audience in the first lines. Historical records list kings and events.

Some genres are easier to identify than others. Satire, for example, is often tricky. Think of how many people post articles on social media from satirical news websites without realizing they aren't true—and those are articles from our own time and place! Bible readers have even more difficulty identifying certain genres because of our lack of familiarity with the social and literary conventions of biblical societies.

Because of those barriers, we often must rely on biblical scholars who have researched other ancient writings to help us identify genre. However, you don't have to become experts in the forms of biblical case law to understand the Ten Commandments. The important thing is to simply recognize that genre matters and know how to investigate biblical genres.

What Is the Bible, Anyway?

What kind of book is the Bible? Or, more accurately, what kinds of books are in the Bible? In which sections of a bookstore or a library do you think you would find each book of the Bible, if they were separated?

These questions are all about genre, or the category to which a piece of writing belongs. We can tell a book's genre

14

EXPLORE

○ Open It Up
○ Foundations

STUDY

○ Read a Text
○ Biblical Tools

by reading it carefully and looking for clues. Just as today we know a story that starts out "Once upon a time . . ." is likely to be a fairy tale, in biblical times, authors had their own ways of signaling which genre they were using.

Why does it matter what genre a book is? Well, knowing the genre of a book can completely change our interpretation of it. For example, if we thought a fairy tale was a news report, we might become frightened, missing the point of the story. Or, if we thought a list of telephone numbers was a secret code, we might spend hours trying to figure it out. Genre is important because it tells you how to understand and respond to a piece of writing.

TRANSLATING GENRE

Did you know that the original Hebrew text of the Old Testament didn't have vowels, capitalization, punctuation, verse numbers, or formatting?

Vowels and paragraph divisions were added to the Hebrew text between the sixth and tenth centuries—hundreds of years after the original texts were written. The chapter and verse numbers we use today were added in the twelfth century. All the rest of the punctuation—indents, question marks, quotation marks, and everything else—is up to modern translators to decide. These details are important because vocabulary, punctuation, and formatting are major clues to genre.

15

FOUNDATIONS

○ If they haven't already done so, allow time for participants to read "Why Does This Matter?" in the Participant Book. (It is encouraged for participants to read this section before the group meets).

○ Invite participants to read "What is the Bible, Anyway?" and "Translating Genre" in their Participant Book.

○ Invite group members to share their initial responses or questions.

○ Write responses on the white board or a large piece of paper. Revisit these thoughts as you further explore the topic.

○ **ASK:** What kinds of genres do you think are included in the Bible?

REFLECT

○ Respond

○ Discuss

Study

READA TEXT

○ **SAY:** In the original Hebrew text of the Old Testament, there were no vowels, punctuation, verse numbers, or formatting. All of that is added for you by the people who copied and translated the Bible. They had to decide when each sentence and section ended and began, and how to format the text depending on what genre they thought it was.

○ Invite the group to look up Jonah 2 in two translations of the Bible (CEB and KJV).

○ **ASK:** What genre does each translator assign to the passage? How can you tell?

○ Invite the group to try their hand at choosing punctuation and formatting for a biblical text by completing the activity in their Participant Book. Afterwards, invite individuals to share and compare their responses *before looking up* the passage in a Bible.

BIBLICAL TOOLS

○ If you have time, have the group read the entire Book of Jonah. Otherwise, invite participants to read an abridged version: 1:1-6, 11-12, 15 and 17; 2:1 and 10; 3:3-5 and 10; 4:1-11.

Check out Jonah, Chapter 2, in two different translations of the Bible—the Common English Bible and the King James Version.

What differences do you notice between each version? How did each translator communicate the genre of the passage, as he or she saw it? Which interpretation do you agree with?

16

○ **ASK:** What genre do you think the Book of Jonah is? What clues are in the story to let you know?

○ Invite the participants to look up the Book of Jonah in a study Bible and Bible commentary. Typically, possible genres are discussed in the introduction to a book. Also, look up Jonah in a Bible dictionary.

Why don't you give it a try yourself? Without looking it up, take the following text from Jonah 1:7b-10. Add your own punctuation, formatting, and verse numbers. Then compare it to what's printed in your Bible.

THEY CAST LOTS AND THE LOT FELL ON JONAH

SO THEY SAID TO HIM TELL US SINCE YOU'RE THE

CAUSE OF THIS EVIL HAPPENING TO US WHAT

DO YOU DO AND WHERE ARE YOU FROM WHAT'S

YOUR COUNTRY AND OF WHAT PEOPLE ARE YOU

HE SAID TO THEM I'M A HEBREW I WORSHIP

THE LORD THE GOD OF HEAVEN WHO MADE THE

SEA AND THE DRY LAND THEN THE MEN WERE

TERRIFIED AND SAID TO HIM WHAT HAVE YOU

DONE THE MEN KNEW THAT JONAH WAS FLEEING

FROM THE LORD BECAUSE HE HAD TOLD THEM

17

Reflect

RESPOND

○ Invite participants to spend some time in individual reflection, responding to questions in the Participant Book.

DISCUSS

○ Invite the students to share their responses as they feel comfortable.

○ Return to the initial questions and responses written on the white board or large piece of paper. Consider new insights or perspectives. Discuss any remaining questions.

○ **ASK:** Do you believe God still speaks through the Bible, even if the original meaning is lost to us? Why or why not?

○ Invite participants to take home their Participant Books and to read "Why Does This Matter?" for session 3 during the week.

○ **ASK:** What genres do the commentators assign to Jonah? How would your interpretation of the story be different depending on the genre you assume?

○ **SAY:** Study Bibles and Bible commentaries are written by scholars. But remember that commentators are just people, sharing their best interpretations. You bring your own insights and questions to the Bible. It's okay to disagree with a commentary.

Closing Prayer

God of us all, we give thanks for the courage of those gathered here. Inspire our hearts to find you in your Holy Word. May our time together help us live as faithful people in your name. Amen.

Notes

When? Context

Why does this matter?

When children are in grade school, their reading skills improve and they begin to encounter new vocabulary. They're taught to work from the meaning of unfamiliar words by using "context clues." Many adults still do this reflexively, because they know that words can take on different meanings depending on the context. Gross can mean "yucky" when your child says it, but it typically means "the overall total" when it's printed on your paycheck.

The meaning of any given word is dependent on the words around it, because languages are systems. And languages are produced by societies, which are systems of people. The meanings of words, phrases, and whole stories change as society changes. Take the word *nice*. In the fourteenth century, *nice* meant "ignorant" or "foolish." Over hundreds of years, the word has changed meanings several times, landing on "agreeable." An insult has become a compliment.

When modern readers encounter a biblical text, contexts collide. It's easy to forget that the Bible was created in another language and society when today, we're reading the Bible on our cell phones. Most modern readers bring their own linguistic and cultural understandings to bear on the Bible without even realizing that they are doing so. People only tend to remember the contextual divide between themselves and the text when the stories are strange or archaic. When this happens, they can't seamlessly absorb them into their modern worldview.

The truth is, context always matters in interpretation, whether or not the reader is aware of it. Anytime someone picks up the Bible, there are at least three contexts to consider—the literary context, the historical context, and the cultural context. We are already familiar with our own cultural context. How do we become familiar with the literary and historical contexts of the Bible?

Historians, biblical archaeologists, linguists, and other scholars have done the research. Bible dictionaries, commentaries, and handbooks contain condensed versions of that research. Using these tools, you can discover the biblical "context clues" that shed new light on texts.

Supplies

- study Bibles (CEB)
- Bible dictionary (CEB)
- Bible commentary
- Bible handbook
- Participant Book
- dry-erase board and marker set or large piece of paper
- pens, pencils, colored pencils, markers

Learning Goals

- Deepen understandings of the connection between context and meaning
- Compare biblical and modern cultural contexts
- Use Bible dictionaries, commentaries, and handbooks to research biblical context

Helping Participants

You may think you need to have all the answers in order to do an in-depth Bible study. I've got good news for you: you don't! In fact, it is likely people prefer it if you avoid giving the answers. Instead, let participants explore and come to their own understandings. Your job is to ask good questions, facilitate conversation, and to help keep the group on track.

Some group members will have had the benefit of cross-cultural experiences in their life; others may have not. Cultural assumptions are usually taken for granted until another culture is encountered. The Bible brings another culture into the room, and is ripe for cross-cultural encounter if we allow it to unfold. Help participants have curiosity about life in biblical times and the meaning of the stories to their original audiences.

Explore

OPEN IT UP

○ Before class, download "Context Clues" pictures http://www.deepbluekids.com/learningtostudy. Print the pictures and cut them apart.

○ One at a time, go through the cards with the group. Invite the participants to try to identify what they are looking at in each picture. (Each card is a real photograph. Cover the answer in the bottom corner with your finger.)

○ **ASK:** Which card was the easiest to identify? Which was the hardest? Why?

○ **SAY:** When you're trying to identify something, it helps to see its context—what's around it. It's the same with words, ideas, and stories. When we interpret the Bible, understanding context is very important.

When modern readers encounter a biblical text, contexts collide. It's easy to forget that the Bible was created in another language and society when today we're reading the Bible on our cell phones. Most modern readers bring our own linguistic and cultural understandings to bear on the Bible without even realizing that we are doing so. We only tend to remember the contextual divide between ourselves and the text when the stories are strange or archaic. When this happens, we can't seamlessly absorb them into our modern worldview.

The truth is, context always matters in interpretation, whether or not the reader is aware of it. Anytime someone picks up the Bible, there are at least three contexts to consider—the literary context, the historical context, and the cultural context. We are already familiar with our own cultural context. How do we become familiar with the literary and historical contexts of the Bible?

Historians, biblical archaeologists, linguists, and other scholars have done the research. Bible dictionaries, commentaries, and handbooks contain condensed versions of that research. Using these tools, we can discover the context clues that shed new light on biblical texts.

22

EXPLORE

○ Open It Up
○ Foundations

STUDY

○ Read a Text
○ Biblical Tools

CONTEXTUALIZE IT

context (noun) \kän-tekst\ | the group of conditions that exist where and when something happens. From the Latin contextere, "to weave together."

What's up? What's down? What's going on around you? Are you a person walking on the sidewalk? Are you a bird flying in the air? Are you an alien living on another planet? Whatever is happening in your world, whatever circumstances affect your everyday life, that's your historical context.

In most American cities, our context includes things like:

- the fact that we can take a car, bus, bike, or walk to work;
- the ability to instantly get in touch with people hundreds of miles away through email, phones, and social media;
- the fact that most of us in our community learn how to read; and
- the ability to buy fresh fruits and vegetables from the grocery store year-round.

These realities are so common that many people don't realize that they haven't always been true, and still aren't true in every culture. For most people, their context feels like the way things should be. They don't even realize there's another way of doing things until they meet someone from another culture or experience the other culture themselves.

23

REFLECT

○ Respond

○ Discuss

FOUNDATIONS

○ If they haven't already done so, allow time for participants to read "Why Does This Matter?" in the Participant Book. (It is encouraged for participants to read this section before the group meets).

○ Read, "Contextualize It" in the Participant book.

○ Invite group members to share their initial responses or questions. Write responses on the white board or a large piece of paper. Revisit these thoughts as you further explore the topic.

○ **ASK:** What do you think a person from Bible times would say if they were a part of our world? What might surprise them?

○ Invite the group to complete the Alien Archaeologist activity in the Participant Book (see page 25).

○ Invite group members to share their responses.

○ **ASK:** What other objects might be confusing to an alien archaeologist? How is the Alien Archaeologist game similar to the research of biblical archaeologists?

Study

READ A TEXT

○ Invite participants to read "Before and After" in the Participant Book.

○ Have them look up Luke 6:1-11 in their Bibles and read the story out loud.

○ On the white board or large piece of paper, write down observations or questions.

BIBLICAL TOOLS

○ Divide the participants into two groups. Have one group read the section before (Luke 5:33-39) and one group read the section after the passage (Luke 6:12-19). Have each group record their observations.

○ **ASK:** How is this passage connected to what comes before it? To what comes after it? Does knowing what comes before and after the story affect your interpretation? Why or why not?

○ Invite the group to explore questions using study Bibles, commentaries, and Bible dictionaries.

○ Go back to the initial observations and questions and compare it to the information gathered.

When we read the Bible, we're like time travelers entering another culture. We're reading stories, prophecies, and letters from completely different contexts, passed down to us through hundreds of years. Nobody reading the Bible today remembers what it was like to live in Jerusalem when King David ruled, or in Persia when Esther was queen, or in Nazareth when Jesus was growing up.

So, when we read the Bible today, we have to work to contextualize it. We have to put the story back into its own context. First, we learn about the time and place, when and where the story was written, so we can understand what it might have meant at the time. We also put the story in its literary context by reading what comes before and after the story. Then, we can think about what it might mean today, in our own context.

24

Alien Archaeologist

Imagine you are an alien from a distant planet. You've landed on planet Earth. You begin exploring and encounter the following objects/items. From your alien context, write what you think each item might be for. Remember, as an alien, you know absolutely NOTHING about human culture.

Hair Dryer—

Carousel—

Vacuum Cleaner—

Fishing Pole—

Clothes Hanger—

25

Reflect

RESPOND

○ Invite participants to spend some time in individual reflection, responding to questions in the Participant Book.

DISCUSS

○ Invite the students to share their responses as they feel comfortable.

○ Return to the initial questions and responses written on the white board or large piece of paper. Consider new insights or perspectives. Discuss any remaining questions.

○ **ASK:** Why does the historical context of the Bible matter? What difference does it make?

○ Invite participants to take home their Participant Books and to read "Why Does This Matter?" for session 4 during the week.

Closing Prayer

Holy God, as we wander through your word help us to seek and find you. You are the meaning maker of our lives, and it is through your word we discover new ways of living as your faithful people. Amen.

Notes

Where? Geography

Why does this matter?

When it snows in Texas, everything closes. When it snows in Massachusetts, it's business as usual. When urbanites in New York talk about the weather, they're making small talk. When farmers in Kansas talk about the weather, they're talking about work. When it's windy in North Carolina, it makes for a nice breeze. When it's windy in Oklahoma, it could be dangerous. Everyone's life is shaped, to varying degrees, by their geography.

Modern city dwelling folks are less likely to be aware of the effects of geography, but people in Bible times were sharply aware of their relationship with the land. For them, geography was a life-and-death subject, not a subject in school. People in Bible times didn't have maps as we know them, scaled guides of the local landscape. Without a bird's-eye view, the biblical authors' only way of knowing their geography was to explore it and occasionally get lost in it.

Long trips were inherently dangerous, because the prospect of becoming lost without access to food or water was real. Food preservation was difficult, so travelers relied almost entirely on the hospitality of strangers to feed and shelter them. For long trips or moves, people traveled in large family groups and brought their livestock with them. Travel was arduous. In short, being away from or without your own plot of arable land made you vulnerable.

Even when the Israelites did settle in Canaan, their survival was not guaranteed. Long droughts like the one in 1 Kings 17-18 threatened the Israelites' survival. No wonder the Israelites placed such spiritual and religious value on the land as God's promised blessing. The land was life. The poignancy is gone from many modern people's relationship with the land. As a result, we often overlook geography. Imagining the biblical landscape enriches our ability to enter into the biblical narrative. Stories become more textured when we imagine the sensory experience of wandering in the desert or sailing on the Mediterranean. We better understand the urgency of Mary and Joseph's flight to Egypt, or the passion that the magi must have felt to travel all that way. In short, biblical geography reveals a new layer of meaning.

Supplies

- study Bibles (CEB)
- Bible atlas
- Bible dictionaries
- Participant Book
- dry-erase board and marker set or large piece of paper
- pens, pencils, colored pencils, markers
- white paper

Learning Goals

- Discover information about biblical landscape
- Prompt reflection on the relationship between land and daily life
- Use archaeological research and biblical maps to explore biblical geography

Helping Participants

You may think you need to have all the answers in order to do an in-depth Bible study. I've got good news for you: you don't! In fact, it is likely people prefer it if you avoid giving the answers. Instead, let participants explore and come to their own understandings. Your job is to ask good questions, facilitate conversation, and to help keep the group on track.

Some group members may hunt or farm, or have relatives who do so. Others have experience hiking, camping, and learning wilderness survival skills. Others have next to no experience with the outdoors. Persons who have spent time in the wild may have more appreciation for the relationship between geography, survival, and culture. Whatever their experience level, all can benefit from exploring biblical geography. Biblical geography can help visual and sensory learners engage with the stories, and shed new light on well-known narratives.

Explore

OPEN IT UP

○ As people arrive, invite group members to draw a map or write down the directions of their daily commute or a familiar drive.

○ **ASK:** What details did you decide to include on your map? What influenced your decision?

○ Follow up the conversation by inviting group members to share a time when they were traveling and got lost.

○ **ASK:** How did you find your way back?

○ **SAY:** In biblical times, maps drawn to scale didn't exist. It was easy to get lost, so they had to know how to survive from the land. Geography was a life-or-death situation in biblical times.

Long trips were inherently dangerous, because the prospect of becoming lost without access to food or water was real. Food preservation was difficult, so travelers relied almost entirely on the hospitality of strangers to feed and shelter them. For long trips or moves, people traveled in large family groups and brought their livestock with them. Travel was arduous. In short, being away from or without your own plot of arable land made you vulnerable.

Even when the Israelites did settle in Canaan, their survival was not guaranteed. Long droughts like the one in 1 Kings 17-18 threatened the Israelites' survival. No wonder the Israelites placed such spiritual and religious value on the land as God's promised blessing. The land was life. Today, this poignancy is gone from many modern people's relationship with the land. As a result, we often overlook geography. Imagining the biblical landscape enriches our ability to enter into the biblical narrative. Stories become more textured when we imagine the sensory experience of wandering in the desert or sailing on the Mediterranean. We better understand the urgency of Mary and Joseph's flight to Egypt, or the passion that the magi must have felt to travel all that way. In short, biblical geography reveals a new layer of meaning.

BIBLE GEOGRAPHY

When you hear the word geography, what do you think? If you're like most people, you think of maps. But geography is about much more than national borders or navigation.

EXPLORE

○ Open It Up
○ Foundations

STUDY

○ Read a Text
○ Biblical Tools

Where? Geography

The geography, or landscape, of your homeland shapes your life in important ways. Your local geography determines the food you eat, the clothes you wear, the type of house you live in, and more.

Now that we live in a globally connected world, we're not completely limited by our geography. We can eat a banana grown in Jamaica, pull on a T-shirt made in Cambodia, and ride in a car made in Japan—all before we go to work. Even so, it's likely that if you live on the Maine coast, seafood is a regular part of your diet; and if you live in Alaska, you own a heavy coat; and if you live in Kansas, you know where to take shelter during a tornado.

How much our geography affects us differs, depending on where we live. But in biblical times, geography played a much bigger role in people's lives. Their lives were determined by their local geography. They ate whatever food they could grow or raise on the land. They wore whatever clothing they could make from local plants or animal skins. They built houses out of bricks made from local mud or stone.

Most of the stories in the Bible take place in Israel, a small land, but packed with diversity. The land of ancient Israel contained high mountains (Mount Hermon is 9,000 feet!) as well as the Dead Sea, the lowest point on the earth's surface. Parts of Israel were dry and desert-like, and other parts were humid and close to the Mediterranean Sea.

Wheat, barley, figs, pistachios, grapes, and olive trees were abundant. The Israelites snacked on bread, olive oil, fruit, and nuts.

31

FOUNDATIONS

○ If they haven't already done so, allow time for participants to read "Why Does This Matter?" in the Participant Book.

○ Read, "Bible Geography" in the Participant book.

○ Invite group members to share their initial responses or questions. Write responses on the white board or a large piece of paper. Revisit these thoughts as you further explore the topic.

○ **ASK:** What parts of your life are the most affected by your local geography?

○ Discuss some times when weather, geography, or landscape have affected our lives.

REFLECT

○ Respond
○ Discuss

Study

READ A TEXT

○ Invite participants to find Exodus 16:1-21 in their Bibles and read the text together.

○ Write questions on a dry-erase board or large piece of paper. If there are few questions, help them along with suggestions. Possibilities include: What food is available in the desert? What is manna? How far is it from Egypt to Canaan? Where is the Reed Sea? How hot was the desert?

BIBLICAL TOOLS

○ Invite the participants to explore their questions using a study Bible, Bible atlas, and Bible dictionaries.

○ **ASK:** What information have you gathered? How does this information shed light on our story? Have some of your questions been answered?

○ **SAY:** Much of the information we have about the geography of the biblical world comes from archaeology.

Sheep and goats were able to survive on the dry, broken terrain, so Israelite clothes were often made from wool or leather.

BIBLICAL TOOLS
- Find Exodus 16:1-21 in the Bible.
- Look up maps using a study Bible and Bible atlas.

How do you think geography might affect the experience the Israelites had wandering in the wilderness? What would you like to find out about the geography of their journey?

What information have you gathered? How does this information shed light on our story?

32

How familiar were you with the biblical landscape before now? What's one thing you learned that you didn't know before?

What does the wilderness symbolize to you? Have you ever been in a spiritual wilderness?

How does learning more about the literal wilderness help you understand the symbolic wilderness? What does this story teach us about being in a wilderness and relying on God?

33

Reflect

RESPOND

○ Invite participants to spend some time in individual reflection, responding to questions in the Participant Book.

DISCUSS

○ Invite the participants to share their responses as they feel comfortable.

○ Return to the initial questions and responses written on the white board or large piece of paper. Consider new insights or perspectives. Discuss any remaining questions.

○ **ASK:** What does geography have to do with biblical interpretation? What difference does it make?

○ Invite participants to take home their Participant Books and to read "Why Does This Matter?" for session 5 during the week.

Closing Prayer

God of promise, whose grace and guidance brought your people from out of the wilderness into a land of promise, we journey alongside you to discover your word for our lives. May we always seek to follow you. Amen.

Notes

Why? Interpretation

Why does this matter?

Interpretation is the work of the human brain. Our brains are constantly at work interpreting the world around us and all forms of communication therein. Imagine two people hiking in the woods. They each see a large, brown form ahead. The first person interprets the shape as a fallen tree trunk, and hardly reacts. The second person interprets the shape as a bear, and quickly becomes frightened. Each person's interpretation of the shape happened in fractions of a second, unconsciously.

When we read the Bible, our brains process the text through its already existing frameworks. These might be called our "interpretive lenses" because they filter information before it even arrives at our conscious brain. This is similar to eyeglass lenses filtering visual images before our brain processes them. It's our job to identify our interpretive lenses and be aware of them as we read the text. Only then will we be able to understand how we can read the same text as another person and then sometimes arrive at opposing interpretations.

In addition to interpretive lenses, there are interpretive layers we must acknowledge. The biblical text arrives in our hands at the end of a centuries-long process of interpretation. Remember, between us and the original audiences of the Bible, there are translators, canonizers, scribes and copyists, editors, authors, and oral storytellers. Each of these represents a separate interpretive layer; each person who wrote, edited, copied, canonized, and translated the text made interpretive decisions.

Through all these layers and lenses, we read the Bible and make meaning from it. The task is, at times, daunting. This is why belief in the guidance of the Holy Spirit in hearing and understanding God's word is so essential. It's also why reading the Bible in community is crucial to faithful interpretation. We read our holy Scriptures in community so that we might hear the interpretation of people in different life situations. Only then can all the facets of God's word come to life. You and your faith community have an important part in the sacredness of interpreting the Bible.

Supplies

- study Bibles (CEB)
- various Bible translations
- Bible commentary
- Bible dictionary (CEB)
- Bible concordance
- Participant Book
- pens, pencils, colored pencils, markers, paper
- dry-erase board and marker set or large piece of paper
- basket

Learning Goals

- Create awareness of interpretive lenses and layers
- Spark curiosity about our own and others' interpretive lenses
- Use a concordance and various translations to compare meanings

Helping Participants

You may think you need to have all the answers in order to do an in-depth Bible study. I've got good news for you: you don't! In fact, it is likely people prefer it if you avoid giving the answers. Instead, let participants explore and come to their own understandings. Your job is to ask good questions, facilitate conversation, and to help keep the group on track

Many people notice how people's life experiences affect how they see the world. Even an example as simple as whether one sees the glass half-full or half-empty will resonate with their lived experience. That lived experience may not naturally translate to the Bible, especially if they've been taught that the Bible has one meaning or interpretation. Introducing the Bible's "interpretive layers" and the long history of differing interpretations might give group members the freedom to add their own voice to the conversation.

Explore

OPEN IT UP

○ Write the following questions on separate pieces of paper. (You may need to write some questions down twice depending on the size of your group.)

Have you ever felt singled out because of race or ethnicity?

Do you feel like there are some activities you should or shouldn't do because of your gender?

Do you have a disability that affects how you move, learn, or interact with others? How does this affect you?

Are you an introvert, extrovert, or in-between? How does this change the way you connect to others?

Do you feel like you have enough, too much, or too little? Why?

Are you the oldest, youngest, middle, or only child? How does this affect the way you relate to your family?

How do you want to spend the majority of your time?

○ As they arrive, have participants draw questions from the basket and write their answers.

○ Once everyone has arrived, invite those who are willing to share their responses.

○ **ASK:** How do these things affect the way you interact with others and the world? How much do you think your life experience affects how you read the Bible? Why?

Only then will we be able to understand how we can read the same text as another person and then sometimes arrive at opposing interpretations.

In addition to interpretive lenses, there are interpretive layers we must acknowledge. The biblical text arrives in our hands at the end of a centuries-long process of interpretation. Remember, between us and the original audiences of the Bible, there are translators, canonizers, scribes and copyists, editors, authors, and oral storytellers. Each of these represents a separate interpretive layer; each person who wrote, edited, copied, canonized, and translated the text made interpretive decisions.

Through all these layers and lenses, we read the Bible and make meaning from it. The task is, at times, daunting. This is why belief in the guidance of the Holy Spirit in hearing and understanding God's word is so essential. It's also why reading the Bible in community is crucial to faithful interpretation. We read our holy Scriptures in community so that we might hear the interpretation of people in different life situations. Only then can all the facets of God's word come to life. You and your faith community have an important part in the sacredness of interpreting the Bible.

We have lots of tools to help us investigate the meaning of biblical passages. In the end, it's up to us to determine, through prayer and reflection, what the Bible means to our lives today.

36

EXPLORE

○ Open It Up
○ Foundations

STUDY

○ Read a Text
○ Biblical Tools

LAYERS AND LENSES

There are layers to interpretation. There are also lenses. Lenses and layers. Layers and lenses. This can get confusing at times. Here's a breakdown of the lenses and layers of Bible interpretation:

Layers

Between the original author and the modern reader, the Bible passed through many hands. By the time the Bible gets to you, it's already gone through several layers of interpretation, which have influenced the meaning.

The Translators—The Bible was originally written in Hebrew, Greek, and occasionally other languages. You can read the Bible in English thanks to the work of translators. If you've ever learned a foreign language, you know that translation can be tricky. Words and phrases in one language don't translate neatly into another. Take the English phrase "I ran into him at the store." If you translated that word-by-word into another language, the reader might imagine someone literally sprinting into another person. In order to get the true meaning across, the translator needs to figure out how to convey the idea of coincidentally meeting someone at the store. Translators have to decide the best way to communicate all kinds of words and phrases in another language, and that's interpretation.

37

FOUNDATIONS

○ If they haven't already done so, allow time for participants to read "Why Does This Matter?" in the Participant Book.

○ Read "Layers and Lenses" in the Participant Book.

○ Invite group members to share their initial responses or questions. Write responses on the white board or a large piece of paper. Revisit these thoughts as you further explore the topic.

○ **ASK:** Which interpretive layer seems the most important to you? Why?

REFLECT

○ Respond

○ Discuss

Study

READAT TEXT

○ Invite the group to take turns reading Genesis 1:1-31 out loud.

○ **SAY:** We're going to do a bit of research to help us understand what it means to be created in God's image. Let's start with the basic questions we've already learned to ask: Who wrote this? What genre is this? When was this written? And where?

○ **SAY:** Did you know that one of the most debated parts of the Bible is in the very first chapter? Genesis 1 is a poem about Creation. The poet says that God created humanity in "God's own image." For centuries, Jews and Christians have tried to understand what that means. What's your interpretation?

○ Invite participants to share their interpretations of the statement: "God created humanity in God's own image" (Genesis 1:27).

○ Write responses on the dry-erase board or a large piece of paper.

BIBLICAL TOOLS

○ Divide the participants into small groups. Have each group use a different tool to investigate the passage (Genesis 1:1-31), choosing between a study Bible, a commentary, a Bible dictionary, and a concordance.

The Canonizers—How did the Bible become the Bible? Why were some stories, letters, and gospels preserved while others faded into obscurity? The answer lies with the canonizers. The canonizers are the people who decided which books were important enough to be in the canon or the Christian Bible, and what order they should go in. Most of the canonizers were Christian leaders during the second to fourth centuries.

The Scribes—Back before the printing press was invented, each copy of the Bible was written by hand by a scribe. Scribes carefully wrote every word exactly as they saw it in their original manuscript. But the scribes were human. Sometimes they made mistakes. Sometimes they intentionally altered the text to make up for what they thought was an error. As archaeologists unearth and historians preserve ancient scrolls, they can compare them to discover the variations.

The Editors—Many of the books of the Bible draw from different sources. The editors of the Bible took many stories—written and passed down orally—and wove them into one story. Biblical scholars can sometimes tell when an editor has combined two stories, because the writing style changes abruptly.

38

○ **ASK:** What information have you gathered? How does this information shed light on our story?

○ **SAY:** We have lots of tools to help us investigate the meaning of biblical passages. In the end, it's up to us to determine, through prayer and reflection, what the Bible means to our lives today.

Lenses

In addition to layers, there are also lenses of interpretation. Everybody wears metaphorical glasses when they read. The "lenses" you read through influence how you interpret the story. Your lenses are shaped by life experiences.

A person who is afraid of storms might read Jesus calming the storm with a different lens then someone who loves the rain. Someone with an anxiety disorder will read Jesus' encouragement not to worry differently than others. Everyone has a different set of lenses. That's why everyone reads the Bible differently.

BIBLICAL TOOLS

Did you know that one of the most debated parts of the Bible is in the very first chapter? Genesis 1 is a poem about Creation. The poet says that God created humanity in "God's own image." For centuries, Jews and Christians have tried to understand what that means. What's your interpretation?

- Read Verse 27, and what comes after it, in Genesis 1:27-31.
- Read it from a few different translations so you have a sense of what the original language could have meant.
- Use a different tool to investigate the passage, choosing between a study Bible, a commentary, a Bible dictionary, and a concordance.

39

Reflect

RESPOND

O Invite participants to spend some time in individual reflection, responding to questions in the Participant Book.

DISCUSS

O Invite group members to share their responses as they feel comfortable.

O Return to the initial questions and responses written on the white board or large piece of paper. Consider new insights or perspectives. Discuss any remaining questions.

O **ASK:** What do lenses and layers have to do with biblical interpretation? What difference do they make?

O Invite participants to take home their Participant Books and to read "Why Does This Matter?" for session 6 during the week.

O Read Verse 27 again.

O **ASK:** What other questions do you have that might help us interpret verse 27?

O Read it from a few different translations so you have a sense of what the original language could have meant.

Closing Prayer

God of the Bible, you have created us as unique children of God. Each of us is held by your holy hands. May we remember to see you in all living things. Your word is a living document which reminds us of your vision for the world. We are thankful. Amen.

Notes

How? Read Closely

Why does this matter?

When we read the Bible today, we have turnable pages or scrollable screens. We can have Bible verses delivered to our email inboxes. We can study the Bible with apps that show us multiple translations at once. Our Bible ease-of-use rating is off the charts. It's hard sometimes to imagine the effort that went into creating these ancient texts. It's even hard for us, who have always lived in a world with printing presses, to imagine the arduous task of copying manuscripts by hand.

In our biblical ancestors' economy of words, each word held much more value than it does now. The people who wrote, edited, and copied the biblical text didn't take a single word for granted. Every word was carefully chosen by authors, copied by scribes, and memorized by illiterate people of faith. When we practice reading the Bible closely, we honor the careful work of our ancestors.

We also strengthen our faith by paying attention. Simone Weil, a French Catholic theologian, argued that prayer is the highest form of paying attention, of opening oneself to God. Any lesser form of paying attention, such as studying the Bible, only strengthens one's ability to pay attention in prayer.

Many of us read the Bible and begin drawing conclusions about the meaning before we even finish reading. This tendency to interpret on autopilot impedes the process of paying close attention to a text. Why would we need to read it carefully if we already know what it means?

Christians who read the Bible carefully are often surprised by what they find. For example, in nearly every nativity set there are three magi figures. If most Christians were asked why, they'd respond that the Bible says three magi visited Jesus. But the Bible doesn't say there were three magi. Much of what we assume the Bible says comes from our cultural Christian traditions. This is a small example. In other instances, a failure to read carefully might yield a more drastic difference in interpretation. The goal is to slow down and read carefully by paying attention to the four possible meanings, or "senses," that Jewish and Christian interpreters have historically looked for in the biblical text.

Supplies

- ⃝ study Bibles (CEB)
- ⃝ Bible dictionary (CEB)
- ⃝ Bible concordance
- ⃝ pens, pencils, colored pencils, markers
- ⃝ white paper
- ⃝ dry-erase board and marker set or large piece of paper
- ⃝ Participant Book

Learning Goals

- ⃝ Cultivate appreciation for our ancestors' preservation of the biblical text
- ⃝ Practice reading carefully
- ⃝ Discover the four senses of Scripture and practice interpreting them

Helping Participants

You may think you need to have all the answers in order to do an in-depth Bible study. I've got good news for you: you don't! In fact, it is likely people prefer it if you avoid giving the answers. Instead, let participants explore and come to their own understandings. Your job is to ask good questions, facilitate conversation, and to help keep the group on track

Interpreting the Bible according to four senses, or meanings, is an ancient practice. Today, people of faith often present only two options for interpreting Scripture: literally, or figuratively. Strict literalists often give the impression that there is only one "right" interpretation of Scripture; strictly figurative readers often dilute the bold claims of Scripture to the point of truisms. Neither approach helps persons apply the Scriptures to their lives. The four senses of Scripture are an interpretive framework that allows us to take the Scriptures seriously, while not limiting them to their literal sense. Often Scriptures that are difficult to apply in their literal sense are rich in symbolic, allegorical, or comparative meanings.

Explore

OPEN IT UP

○ Make white paper and colored pencils available. Give the group five minutes to recreate, in the most detail possible, an accurate drawing or verbal description of a dollar bill. They should represent both sides of the bill. Don't allow looking at a bill for reference.

○ After the time is up, compare the drawings or verbal descriptions with a real dollar bill. Discuss what they were able to depict accurately, what they drew or described inaccurately, and what they left out entirely.

○ **SAY:** You have seen a dollar bill countless times before this. Yet, just because something is very familiar to us, that doesn't mean we pay close attention to it. The Bible is the same way. We may have heard Bible stories dozens of times, but might never have read them carefully.

We also strengthen our faith by paying attention. Simone Weil, a French Catholic theologian, argued that prayer is the highest form of paying attention, of opening oneself to God. Any lesser form of paying attention, such as studying the Bible, only strengthens one's ability to pay attention in prayer.

Many of us read the Bible and begin drawing conclusions about the meaning before we even finish reading. This tendency to interpret on autopilot impedes the process of paying close attention to a text. Why would we need to read it carefully if we already know what it means?

Christians who read the Bible carefully are often surprised by what they find. For example, in nearly every nativity set there are three magi figures. If most Christians were asked why, they'd respond that the Bible says three magi visited Jesus. But the Bible doesn't say there were three magi. Much of what we assume the Bible says comes from our cultural Christian traditions. This is a small example. In other instances, a failure to read carefully might yield a more drastic difference in interpretation. The goal is to slow down and read carefully by paying attention to the four possible meanings, or "senses," that Jewish and Christian interpreters have historically looked for in the biblical text.

44

EXPLORE

○ Open It Up
○ Foundations

STUDY

○ Read a Text
○ Biblical Tools

FOUR MEANINGS, ONE TEXT

How many different ways can you read one passage of the Bible? Well, since the Middle Ages, some Jewish and Christian Bible interpreters have believed there are at least four ways. Their lists didn't match up perfectly, but each tradition listed four unique ways to interpret Scripture. Here's a mash-up of the two lists:

The literal, or plain meaning—Christian interpreters called this the literal sense. Rabbis called this the *peshat*, from the Hebrew word for "surface." This way of reading takes the text at face value.

The comparative meaning—The comparative meaning is what the meaning passages take on when read in connection with other parts of the Bible. Christian interpreters called this the allegorical or typological sense. Rabbis called this the *derash*, from the Hebrew word for "inquire, seek." This way of reading looks at a passage as a part of the whole Bible, not just by itself.

The deeper symbolic meaning—Christian interpreters called this the moral sense, or the "moral of the story." Rabbis called this the *remez*, from the Hebrew word for "hints." This way of reading looks for meaningful symbols and lessons that can be drawn from the passage.

45

REFLECT

O Respond

O Discuss

FOUNDATIONS

O If they haven't already done so, allow time for participants to read "Why Does This Matter?" in the Participant Book.

O Read, "Four Meanings, One Text" in the Participant Book.

O Invite group members to share their initial responses or questions. Write responses on the white board or a large piece of paper. Revisit these thoughts as you further explore the topic.

O ASK: What do you think of these four ways of reading the Bible? Which one seems the easiest? Which one seems the hardest? Do you think it's possible for these ways of reading the Bible to contradict one another?

O Invite group members to pair up and complete the "Interpret a Fairy Tale" activity in their Participant Books.

O Invite each pair to share their interpretations.

O ASK: Do you think interpreting a fairy tale is easier or harder than interpreting the Bible? Why?

Study

READA TEXT

○ Read Genesis 22:1-19 out loud.

○ Write down "Literal" interpretations on the dry-erase board or large piece of paper.

○ Invite the group to describe literal interpretations and write them on the board or paper.

1. Who is in the story?

2. Where does the story take place?

3. What are the main points of the plot?

4. How does the story end?

○ **SAY:** Now let's add the headings "Comparative" and "Symbolic" and tackle the meanings of the story.

BIBLICAL TOOLS

○ Divide participants into two groups.

○ Have one group investigate the comparative meaning of the story by looking up the related passages listed in a study Bible (these are usually found in the margin). They might also look up interesting words in the concordance to see how they are used elsewhere.

The secret, mystical meaning—Christian interpreters called this the anagogical sense. They believed some passages contained hidden prophecies about heaven, hell, and the second coming of Christ. Rabbis called this the *sod*, from the Hebrew word for "secret." They believed this meaning of the text could only be revealed to a reader through divine inspiration.

INTERPRET A FAIRY TALE

Let's try out the first three forms of interpretation with a common story—"Little Red Riding Hood." If it's been a while since you've heard the story, here's a recap:

Little Red Riding Hood is a little girl named after the fancy, red cloak she wears. One day, her mother sends her to visit her granny with a basket of food. Her mother warns her to stay on the path through the forest.

A Big Bad Wolf is also in the forest. He spies Red and follows her for a while. He approaches her and asks her where she's going. Red tells the Wolf she's visiting her granny. The Wolf suggests that she pick some flowers for Granny. While Red is picking flowers, the Wolf goes ahead of her and eats her granny!

The Wolf puts on Granny's clothes and waits for Red to arrive. Red notices immediately how different Granny looks. She comments, "My, what big eyes you have!" The Wolf responds, "The better to see you with, my dear." Red says, "My, what big ears you have!" The Wolf responds, "The better to hear you with, my dear." Red exclaims, "My, what big teeth you have!" The Wolf growls, "The better to eat you with!"

46

○ Have the other group investigate the symbolic meaning of the story by reading the notes in a study Bible and looking up potential symbols in a Bible dictionary.

○ Have each group write their findings on the dry-erase board or large piece of paper next to "Literal" and under the appropriate headings, "Comparative" and "Symbolic."

Then he proceeds to eat Red as well. Fortunately, a hunter drops by, cuts open the Big Bad Wolf, and rescues Little Red Riding Hood and her granny.

TRY IT OUT:

- Literal meaning—tell the story in your own words.
- Comparative meaning—are there any connections between this story and other fairy tales? Do Big Bad Wolves appear in other stories? What about young girls? Grandmothers? Forests? Think of all the connections you can.
- Symbolic meaning—What's the "moral of the story?" What are the symbols in the story? What do they represent?

When you're interpreting the literal sense of a biblical passage, you can feel like you are stating the obvious. That's okay! It's an important part of Bible study. Because the truth is, most of the time the literal meaning of the text is obvious. But sometimes it isn't. It's always good to check for a basic level of understanding by restating the main points of the passage in your own words.

47

○ **ASK:** Which of these meanings makes the most sense to you? Why do you think Jewish and Christian interpreters came up with these four ways of looking at a story?

Reflect

RESPOND

○ Invite participants to spend some time in individual reflection, responding to questions in the Participant Book.

DISCUSS

○ Invite group members to share their responses as they feel comfortable.

○ Return to the initial questions and responses written on the white board or large piece of paper. Consider new insights or perspectives. Discuss any remaining questions.

○ **ASK:** How do you think you have interpreted the Bible in the past? How do these new findings affect your reading of Scripture?

○ Invite participants to take home their Participant Books and to read "Why Does This Matter?" for session 7 during the week.

Closing Prayer

Mighty God, you are bigger than anything we can imagine. Yet, your wisdom and your teachings give us a glimpse into who you are and how we can deeply connect to you and to one another. Amen.

Notes

How? Reread

Why does this matter?

The first six lessons of this study teach us how to analyze the Bible by drawing on the findings of historical criticism, literary analysis, biblical archaeology, and more. Those methods of study are invaluable to the modern reader. Those methods also illuminate the biblical text by clarifying its origins, decentering our modern point of view, and drawing us into the strange and exciting world of the original authors and audiences. By studying our ancestors' encounters with God, we open ourselves to our own encounters with God.

Now it's time to turn our focus away from the world of the authors and toward our own responses as readers. Reader-response criticism is a method of interpretation that centers the reader's experience of a text and role in meaning making. Reader-response criticism balances our focus on the original authors of the Bible, alongside the vital role of the reader.

If the biblical text is the "living word of God," then its meaning cannot stagnate in ancient Israel. It must also be capable of making new meaning as people of faith experience the text. Both the historical context and the reader's context are important in Biblical interpretation. This belief is not a newfangled theological response to changing times. It is an ancient belief that is fundamental to Christian biblical interpretation. As early as the New Testament, Christians reinterpreted the Hebrew Scriptures in light of their experience of the resurrected Christ.

By the third century, a Christian theologian named Origen taught a method of prayerfully reading the Scriptures through the lens of Christ, as a way to draw closer to God. He called this method "divine reading" or *lectio divina*, and throughout the centuries, Christian monks have distilled the general method into four steps: *lectio* (read), *meditatio* (meditate), *oratio* (pray), and *contemplatio* (contemplate). This basic method has been adapted into various steps for different audiences. It typically involves reading the same Scripture several times in a meditative fashion.

Today we're focusing on what we bring to biblical interpretation. Each of us brings our unique perspective to every passage we interpret. God speaks to each of us through the Bible, so our life experiences are an important part of interpretation.

Supplies

- Bibles (CEB)
- pens, pencils, colored pencils, markers, paper
- various art supplies such as oil pastels, watercolors, colorful paper, modeling clay, and so forth
- candle and matches
- meditation beads (or pony beads, yarn, and scissors)
- Participant Book
- dry-erase board and marker set or a large piece of paper

Learning Goals

- Create awareness of our own roles in making meaning
- Prompt reflection on the nature of Scripture as the "living word of God"
- Practice the ancient tradition of divine reading

Helping Participants

You may think you need to have all the answers in order to do an in-depth Bible study. I've got good news for you: you don't! In fact, it is likely people prefer it if you avoid giving the answers. Instead, let participants explore and come to their own understandings. Your job is to ask good questions, facilitate conversation, and to help keep the group on track

Many people are more comfortable with a scholastic investigation of Scripture than a spiritual encounter with it. Some people may have never engaged in spiritual practices in a group, and their initial reaction may be discomfort. That's okay! Divine reading is a practice, not an achievement. God can still speak to us when we are uncomfortable. Try to trust the process and avoid intervening during silences that may feel uncomfortable. Lighting a candle or playing meditative music can help set a worshipful tone during your practice.

Explore

OPEN IT UP

○ Once everyone has arrived, invite participants to share their favorite Bible verses or Bible stories.

○ **ASK:** Why is this verse or story important to your life? Are there different way to read or understand this biblical text? Do others hear this story or verse in a different way?

○ **SAY:** Today we're focusing on what we bring to biblical interpretation. We bring our own unique perspectives to every passage we interpret. God speaks to each of us through the Bible, so our life experiences are an important part of interpretation.

If the biblical text is the "living word of God," then its meaning cannot stagnate in ancient Israel. It must also be capable of making new meaning as people of faith experience the text. Both the historical context and the reader's context are important in biblical interpretation. This belief is not a newfangled theological response to changing times. It is an ancient belief that is fundamental to Christian biblical interpretation. As early as the New Testament, Christians reinterpreted the Hebrew Scriptures in light of their experience of the resurrected Christ.

By the third century, a Christian theologian named Origen taught a method of prayerfully reading the Scriptures through the lens of Christ, as a way to draw closer to God. He called this method *lectio divina* or "divine reading," and throughout the centuries, Christian monks have distilled the general method into four steps: *lectio* (read), *meditatio* (meditate), *oratio* (pray), and *contemplatio* (contemplate). This basic method has been adapted into various steps for different audiences. It typically involves reading the same Scripture several times in a meditative fashion.

Today we're focusing on what we bring to biblical interpretation. Each of us brings our unique perspective to every passage we interpret. God speaks to each of us through the Bible, so our life experiences are an important part of interpretation.

DIVINE READING

Over the past few weeks, we've learned a lot about how the Bible was created. You've become a modern-day biblical scholar! Now it's time to shift the focus. Let's talk about you.

52

EXPLORE

○ Open It Up
○ Foundations

STUDY

○ Read a Text
○ Biblical Tools

How? Reread

The Bible isn't just about the people who created it. If it were, why would we still be reading it after all these years? The Bible is also about you. It's your sacred story, and it's your life and faith that is affected by how you relate to the Bible.

When you pick up the Bible, you're not just reading about your spiritual ancestors' encounters with God. You're also opening yourself to having your own encounter with God. The Holy Spirit speaks to us in many ways, and one of those ways is through Scripture.

Today we're going to investigate where you are in the biblical story. What is God saying to you through the Bible? How can you grow closer to God and Jesus Christ through reading Scripture?

Read—Read the passage carefully. Notice any words or phrases that stick out in your mind.

Meditate—In this step, let your brain get creative with the passage. As you or someone else reads the passage again, be creative with art supplies, rewrite a verse, or think deeply as you go over the passage in your mind.

Pray—In this step, have a conversation with God. You can read the passage as though you're praying it, or you can simply ask, "God, what are you saying to me through this passage today?"

Contemplate—In this step, listen for God's response to your prayer and meditation. As the passage is read a final time, quiet your mind and be open to any response you sense.

53

FOUNDATIONS

○ If they haven't already done so, allow time for participants to read "Why Does This Matter?" in the Participant Book.

○ Read, "Divine Reading" in the Participant Book.

○ Invite group members to share their initial responses or questions. Write responses on the white board or a large piece of paper. Revisit these thoughts as you further explore the topic.

○ **ASK:** Do you see yourself in the biblical story? Where? Do you see the Bible as your book, or your story? Why or why not?

REFLECT

○ Respond

○ Discuss

Study

READA TEXT

○ Invite the group to find Psalm 139:1-6 in their Bibles.

○ On the dry-erase board or large piece of paper write down the group's reactions to the biblical text.

○ Invite the group members to choose any artistic materials they would like to use during their meditation, prayer, and contemplation of the passage.

BIBLICAL TOOLS

○ Light a candle before you begin. Turn on quiet instrumental music if you like. Invite someone to read Psalm 139:1-6.

○ Once again, read Psalm 139:1-6. Allow a few minutes of silence for the group to use their art supplies to meditate on the passage.

○ Invite someone to read the passage out loud. Allow a few minutes of silence. Invite participants to pray silently about whatever the passage brings up for them as they continue working with the art materials.

○ Give each person a set of meditation beads. (You can easily make meditation beads by stringing yarn with eight to ten

We have lots of tools to help us develop deeper meaning of biblical passages. In the end, it's up to us to determine, through prayer and reflection, what the Bible means to our lives today.

BIBLICAL TOOLS

- Practice *Lectio Divina*. Choose some artistic materials you would like to use during meditation, prayer, and contemplation of the passage.
- Find Psalm 139:1-6 in your Bible.
- Light a candle before you begin. Turn on quiet instrumental music if you choose.
- Read the passage out loud. Allow a few minutes of silence and use your art supplies to meditate on the passage.
- Read the passage again. Allow a few minutes of silence. Pray about whatever the passage brings up for you.
- Acquire a set of meditation beads. (You can easily make meditation beads by stringing yarn with eight to ten pony beads and knotting each end.)
- During this last reading, we will listen for God to speak to us through the passage. Listening in silence can be a difficult task for busy minds. Meditation beads give our hands something to do as we listen quietly.

54

pony beads and knotting each end.)

○ **SAY:** During this last reading, we will be contemplating the Scripture, or listening for God to speak to us through the passage. Listening in silence can

be a difficult task for busy minds. Meditation beads give our hands something to do as we listen quietly.

How? Reread

What part of the passage "shimmered" or stuck out to you?

What was the easiest part of that reading for you? What was difficult for you? What insights did you gain from this way of reading Scripture?

What did you hear from God as you practiced divine reading today? How will you respond to what you heard?

What does divine reading have to do with biblical interpretation? Where are you in the biblical story?

55

Reflect

RESPOND

○ Invite participants to spend some time in individual reflection, responding to questions in the Participant Book.

DISCUSS

○ Invite group members to share their responses as they feel comfortable.

○ Return to the initial questions and responses written on the white board or large piece of paper. Consider new insights or perspectives. Discuss any remaining questions.

○ **ASK:** Do you believe God speaks to us through the close reading of Scripture? What are other ways God speaks in your life?

○ Invite participants to take home their Participant Books and to read "Why Does This Matter" for session 8 during the week.

○ Invite someone to read the passage out loud. Allow about two minutes of silent contemplation using their meditation beads. To end the time, **SAY:** Amen.

Closing Prayer

God, when we pay close attention to your words, we can find our place in the holy Scriptures. May we remember that this is our story, and if we just listen we can hear your voice calling us to share your story with others. Amen.

Notes

How? Read Together

Why does this matter?

We think of the Bible as one book, because we have the luxury of reading it in bound copies. Even those who study the Bible and recognize it as a collection of disparate texts, created over centuries, tend to speak of the "biblical narrative," or "overarching story of the text." Those may be helpful shorthand ways to refer to our inherited faith, but they don't do justice to the diversity of voices within the biblical canon.

Cohesive narratives are created by one author, or by authors working in concert. The biblical authors didn't have the luxury of checking in with one another to discuss where the enterprise was headed. Some biblical authors clearly had access to other texts that would eventually become part of the Bible. But the collection of texts that make up the canon are piecemeal perspectives on the story of Israel and the Jesus movement that emerged from it. If those who canonized the Scriptures had truly preferred a single, cohesive narrative, they could have omitted books, edited others, and crafted a much smoother story. Instead, they carefully preserved a library of diverse, and at times contradictory, perspectives. Rather than giving us an epic saga, they gave us an opportunity for epic conversation.

We who have inherited bound copies of the "book" known as the Holy Bible have been given an immeasurable gift. We have a bird's-eye view of the sacred stories of our spiritual ancestors. We can see the connections, the comparisons, and the inter-canonical conversations that those who created the text never could have seen. We can weave multiple threads into one larger conversation. But it's important to remember the integrity of each thread on its own. In our eagerness to unearth the "one story" of the Bible, we may find ourselves cutting away threads that seem unnecessary or stubbornly unwilling to be woven into our narrative. We can make the mistake of Martin Luther, who was so convinced that the story of the Bible was "justification by faith alone," he concluded that the Book of James had to go. Rather than glossing over the Bible's dissonant voices, our ancestors invite us to wrestle with them, enter the conversation, and find our own place in the story of faith.

Supplies

- study Bibles (CEB)
- Bible commentary
- Bible dictionary and concordance
- pens, pencils, colored pencils, markers
- dry-erase board and marker set or large piece of paper
- Participant Book

Learning Goals

- Create awareness of the diversity of voices within the canon
- Inspire participants to enter into the centuries-long biblical conversation
- Practice reading the Bible inter-canonically

Helping Participants

You may think you need to have all the answers in order to do an in-depth Bible study. I've got good news for you: you don't! In fact, it is likely people prefer it if you avoid giving the answers. Instead, let participants explore and come to their own understandings. Your job is to ask good questions, facilitate conversation, and to help keep the group on track

For many people right now, faith is a difficult topic. Sometimes, we feel divisive in a controversial conversation; we feel pressured to agree to beliefs we don't entirely understand or agree with. Helping view the Bible as an epic conversation between our spiritual ancestors reframes the conversation. Rather than being asked to agree with an already formed conclusion, participants are invited to join in an epic conversation between people of faith and God.

Explore

OPEN IT UP

○ Once everyone has arrived, invite a group member to begin telling a story. The story does not have to be true. They can simply make it up.

○ After a few moments say "pause" and let the person to his or her right go next. They must add to the story the previous person was telling. After another few moments say "pause" again, and allow the next person to continue the story.

○ Continue creating a story in this fashion until everyone has had a chance to add to the storytelling. The last person should complete the story.

○ SAY: In that game, we created a story by building on what the people before us said. Many of the biblical authors built on what had been written before them. The Bible is like a big conversation. There are all kinds of connections between books. We're going to explore some of those today.

If those who canonized the Scriptures had truly preferred a single, cohesive narrative, they could have omitted books, edited others, and crafted a much smoother story. Instead, they carefully preserved a library of diverse, and at times contradictory, perspectives. Rather than giving us an epic saga, they gave us an opportunity for epic conversation.

We who have inherited bound copies of the "book" known as the Holy Bible have been given an immeasurable gift. We have a bird's-eye view of the sacred stories of our spiritual ancestors. We can see the connections, the comparisons, and the inter-canonical conversations that those who created the text never could have seen. We can weave multiple threads into one larger conversation. But it's important to remember the integrity of each thread on its own. In our eagerness to unearth the "one story" of the Bible, we may find ourselves cutting away threads that seem unnecessary or stubbornly unwilling to be woven into our narrative. We can make the mistake of Martin Luther, who was so convinced that the story of the Bible was "justification by faith alone," he concluded that the Book of James had to go. Rather than glossing over the Bible's dissonant voices, our ancestors invite us to wrestle with them, enter the conversation, and find our own place in the story of faith.

Canon Connections

Back in the days of the early church, being called a "Marcionite" was a big insult. Marcionites followed a man named Marcion, who argued that the teachings of Jesus were completely incompatible with the God of the Old Testament.

58

EXPLORE

○ Open It Up
○ Foundations

STUDY

○ Read a Text
○ Biblical Tools

Thus, he believed that the God of the Old Testament could not be Jesus' father.

Marcion's teachings were rejected by the early church. Even though church leaders recognized some differences between the Hebrew Scriptures and the Gospels, they also saw deep connections. They believed that the teachings of Jesus built upon the teachings in the Hebrew Scriptures. Rather than throwing out the Old Testament, early church leaders reinterpreted it in light of Jesus' Jewish heritage and teachings.

It can be tempting to view the Bible as one epic story, with a plot that perfectly progresses with each book. Marcion thought that's what the Bible should be, so he threw out the parts that didn't match his idea of the biblical story. As we've learned, the Bible is not one big and long story. Instead, the Bible is more like an invitation for an in-depth conversation. There are diverse perspectives, and they don't always easily fit together. But the many voices of the Bible help us understand the many angles of truth.

The parts of the Bible that don't seem to fit are often just another way of looking at the same truth. For many Jews, it didn't seem possible to say that a person was God, or even the Son of God. That concept just didn't fit into their understanding of God. But Christians said that it was possible. They reinterpreted the Hebrew Scriptures in light of Jesus and found new meanings. Can you see both perspectives?

Today, Christians read the New Testament alongside the Old Testament all the time. Some churches follow a

59

FOUNDATIONS

○ If they haven't already done so, allow time for participants to read "Why Does This Matter?" in the Participant Book.

○ Read "Canon Connections" in the Participant Book.

○ Invite group members to share their initial responses or questions. Write responses on the white board or a large piece of paper. Revisit these thoughts as you further explore the topic.

○ **ASK:** Why do you think Marcion's teachings were so appealing to some?

REFLECT

○ Respond

○ Discuss

Study

READ A TEXT

○ Read Psalm 23 and Ezekiel 34:1-16 in the Participant Book.

○ **ASK:** What connections did you see between the Ezekiel passage and the Psalm?

BIBLICAL TOOLS

○ Find John 10:1-16 in the Bible and read the passage together.

○ Divide the participants into small groups and assign characters: the Good Shepherd, the ordinary shepherds, the thieves, the sheep.

○ Invite the groups to write down all the things they can identify about their characters. Gather information using the study Bibles, commentary, Bible dictionary, and concordance.

○ Have each group report their findings. Write them on a dry-erase board or a large piece of paper.

○ **ASK:** How does our knowledge of the Ezekiel passage and Psalm 23 help us understand what Jesus is saying in John 10:1-16?

lectionary. The lectionary always has readings from the Old and New Testaments, because Christians believe the Old and New Testaments talk to each other. Scripture is a conversation, which allows us to explore different parts of that conversation through the lectionary.

Psalm 23 is what you might call a classic. Chances are, you've heard it before. You may even have memorized it when you were younger. Take a moment to refresh your memory:

THE LORD IS MY SHEPHERD

¹The LORD is my shepherd.
    I lack nothing.
²He lets me rest in grassy meadows;
    he leads me to restful waters;
        ³he keeps me alive.
 He guides me in proper paths
    for the sake of his good name.
⁴Even when I walk
    through the darkest valley,
    I fear no danger because you are with me.
Your rod and your staff—
    they protect me.
⁵You set a table for me
    right in front of my enemies.
You bathe my head in oil;
    my cup is so full it spills over!
⁶Yes, goodness and faithful love
    will pursue me all the days of my life,
    and I will live in the LORD's house
    as long as I live.

60

How? Read Together

Did you know that one of the prophets sampled from Psalm 23? Ezekiel 34:1-16 uses this image of God as Israel's shepherd to speak out against unjust leaders. Check out verses 11-16.

[11]The LORD God proclaims: I myself will search for my flock and seek them out. [12]As a shepherd seeks out the flock when some in the flock have been scattered, so will I seek out my flock. I will rescue them from all the places where they were scattered during the time of clouds and thick darkness. [13]I will gather and lead them out from the countries and peoples, and I will bring them to their own fertile land. I will feed them on Israel's highlands, along the riverbeds, and in all the inhabited places. [14]I will feed them in good pasture, and their sheepfold will be there, on Israel's lofty highlands. On Israel's highlands, they will lie down in a secure fold and feed on green pastures. [15]I myself will feed my flock and make them lie down. This is what the LORD God says. [16]I will seek out the lost, bring back the strays, bind up the wounded, and strengthen the weak. But the fat and the strong I will destroy, because I will tend my sheep with justice.

61

Reflect

RESPOND

O Invite participants to spend some time in individual reflection, responding to questions in the Participant Book.

DISCUSS

O Invite group members to share their responses as they feel comfortable.

O Return to the initial questions and responses written on the white board or large piece of paper. Consider new insights or perspectives. Discuss any remaining questions.

O **ASK:** What do you think is the most important message given to us through the voices of our biblical ancestors?

Closing Prayer

God who is still speaking, may we remember to be in continuous conversation with you. Help us to find ourselves in the ongoing biblical conversation so that we may find truth, knowledge, and wisdom on our journey with you. Amen.

Notes